CAMBRIDGE LIBRARY COLLECTION

Books of enduring scholarly value

Religion

For centuries, scripture and theology were the focus of prodigious amounts of scholarship and publishing, dominated in the English-speaking world by the work of Protestant Christians. Enlightenment philosophy and science, anthropology, ethnology and the colonial experience all brought new perspectives, lively debates and heated controversies to the study of religion and its role in the world, many of which continue to this day. This series explores the editing and interpretation of religious texts, the history of religious ideas and institutions, and not least the encounter between religion and science.

A Tract of Plutarch on the Advantage to Be Derived from One's Enemies

Eberhard Nestle (1851–1913) was a German biblical scholar and theologian who studied at the University of Tübingen before teaching in London and across Germany. A talented linguist and textual critic, he published a grammar of Syriac and several editions of ancient manuscripts including the New Testament in Greek. This work, originally published in 1894 as part of the Studia Sinaitica series, is the text in Syriac of a treatise by Plutarch on human virtue found in a manuscript in the library of the Monastery of St Catherine on Mount Sinai. Nestle believed the text dated from the late sixth century and suggested that it was translated into Syriac from Greek by a Christian scholar who adapted it for a Christian audience. This text will be of great interest both to Syriac scholars and to those interested in the comparison of Greek philosophy and Christian theology.

T0364264

Cambridge University Press has long been a pioneer in the reissuing of out-of-print titles from its own backlist, producing digital reprints of books that are still sought after by scholars and students but could not be reprinted economically using traditional technology. The Cambridge Library Collection extends this activity to a wider range of books which are still of importance to researchers and professionals, either for the source material they contain, or as landmarks in the history of their academic discipline.

Drawing from the world-renowned collections in the Cambridge University Library and other partner libraries, and guided by the advice of experts in each subject area, Cambridge University Press is using state-of-the-art scanning machines in its own Printing House to capture the content of each book selected for inclusion. The files are processed to give a consistently clear, crisp image, and the books finished to the high quality standard for which the Press is recognised around the world. The latest print-on-demand technology ensures that the books will remain available indefinitely, and that orders for single or multiple copies can quickly be supplied.

The Cambridge Library Collection brings back to life books of enduring scholarly value (including out-of-copyright works originally issued by other publishers) across a wide range of disciplines in the humanities and social sciences and in science and technology.

A Tract of Plutarch
on the Advantage
to Be Derived
from One's Enemies

The Syriac Version

EDITED AND TRANSLATED BY
EBERHARD NESTLE

CAMBRIDGE
UNIVERSITY PRESS

CAMBRIDGE UNIVERSITY PRESS

Cambridge, New York, Melbourne, Madrid, Cape Town,
Singapore, São Paolo, Delhi, Mexico City

Published in the United States of America by Cambridge University Press, New York

www.cambridge.org
Information on this title: www.cambridge.org/9781108043175

© in this compilation Cambridge University Press 2012

This edition first published 1894
This digitally printed version 2012

ISBN 978-1-108-04317-5 Paperback

A TRACT

OF

PLUTARCH

London: C. J. CLAY AND SONS,
CAMBRIDGE UNIVERSITY PRESS WAREHOUSE,
AVE MARIA LANE.
Glasgow: 263, ARGYLE STREET.

Cambridge: DEIGHTON, BELL AND CO.
Leipzig: F. A. BROCKHAUS.
New York: MACMILLAN AND CO.

STUDIA SINAITICA No. IV.

A TRACT

OF

PLUTARCH

ON THE ADVANTAGE TO BE DERIVED
FROM ONE'S ENEMIES

(DE CAPIENDA EX INIMICIS UTILITATE)

THE SYRIAC VERSION

EDITED FROM A MS. ON MOUNT SINAI

WITH A TRANSLATION AND CRITICAL NOTES

BY

EBERHARD NESTLE, Ph.D., Th.Lic.

LONDON:

C. J. CLAY AND SONS,

CAMBRIDGE UNIVERSITY PRESS WAREHOUSE
AVE MARIA LANE.

1894

Cambridge:

PRINTED BY C. J. CLAY, M.A., AND SONS,

AT THE UNIVERSITY PRESS.

PREFACE.

THE same Syriac manuscript of the Sinaitic Convent (No. 16). which has preserved for us the version of the *Apology of Aristides*, contains also the Syriac translation of *three moral tracts* of *Plutarch*. Two of them have already been printed in Syriac by *de Lagarde* in his Analecta Syriaca; the lost one *de exercitatione*, which has been translated by *Gildemeister* and *Bücheler* (Rheinisches Museum, 1872, vol. 27), and περὶ ἀοργησίας, on which *V. Ryssel* may be compared (über den textkritischen Werth der syrischen Uebersetzungen griechischer Klassiker, II. Theil, Leipzig, 1881, p. 55, 56). The present one does not seem to be found in any of the Syriac MSS. of our European libraries. It stands in the Sinaitic MS. immediately after the Apology of Aristides, before the tract περὶ ἀσκήσεως; it occupies there the fol. 105*a* to 112*a*. For the description of the MS., which is believed to be of the seventh or according to Prof. Sachau of the second part of the sixth century, see the edition of Aristides by J. Rendel Harris and J. Armitage Robinson (Texts and Studies, Cambridge, Vol. I. No. 1 (1891), p. 3—6 of the first edition and the facsimile facing the title page). "The book is made up of a number of separate treatises, all of which are ethical in character." As the discoverer of the Syriac Aristides justly remarked "it was apparently the ethical character of the Apology of Aristides, that secured its

incorporation with the volume," so we may say the same
of the translation and preservation of these moral tracts
of Plutarch.

Surprising as it seems at the first, that Syriac monks
or clerics should have thought of translating into their
mother tongue the writings of a Greek heathen author,
the fact is easily explained if we consider the character
of the writings, which they chose for translation, and the
way in which they made them familiar to their country-
men.   For they are all moral tracts warning against anger
and hatred and recommending love and moderation and
self-restraint.   And it is not a literal translation which
we have here, but *rather an adaptation of the heathen tracts*
for the benefit of the Christian community; all that for
the Christian reader was void of interest or which he could
not approve of, for instance the particulars of Greek mythology, is left out or changed.   If, in consequence of this
character, these Syriac texts are less instructive for the
philological student whose delight is in a most literal
translation of an ancient text, they are all the more inte-
resting for the theological and Christian reader, who finds
here one more link between Grecian philosophy and
Christian piety.   It was the same sound of a truly human
religion which those Syrian scholars heard in the Proverbs
of the Old Testament, in the Sermon on the Mount with
its golden rule or in the Epistle of St James in the New
Testament, and which they also seemed to hear from these
writings of the Greek philosopher, and therefore they made
them accessible to their co-religionists.

But there is a third point which makes the publication
of the following text desirable.   The state of Syriac phi-
lology and lexicography is still such, that every addition
to our stock of printed Syriac texts is highly welcome.
I therefore gladly undertook the task of preparing the

following pages for the press, when Prof. J. Rendel Harris had the great kindness of offering me, for this purpose, the copy which he had made from the MS. on Mount Sinai. A few remarks, I hope, will be sufficient.

The Syriac text is printed from the very copy made by Prof. Harris; but where an alteration seemed to be necessary, the emendation was received into the text and the reading of Prof. Harris always given in the margin. Prof. Harris has also corrected my printed text by the aid of photographs. As a rule the text is well preserved and the translation very fluent and easy. There are passages which read more smoothly in Syriac than in the original Greek, just as it is for instance with the book of Titus of Bostra against the Manicheans and its Syriac version. There are, however, some points in the text, on which a remark seems desirable.

p. 1, l. 5. The interpunction is to be changed; ܐܢܬ ܒܩܘܠܣܘܢ begins the apodosis.

p. 1, l. 7. As the text stands, the translation must be: there is not to be found *in the land of Creta what is called a wild beast*; but should we not expect: in the land that is called Creta?

p. 1, l. 21. ܘܗܪܐ ܗܘܐ ܒܠܥܘܪ ܢܚܝ ܗܘܐ ܠܗܘܢ ܚܙܘ ܕܚܘܬܪܐ. Here the construction of the feminine subject ܗܪܐ ܗܘܬ with the masculine predicate ܢܚܝ ܗܘܐ is irregular,—we expect ܗܘܬ ܢܚܝܐ or ܗܘܬ ܢܚܝܐ; and if we consider the first ܗܘܬ as the enclitic ܗܘܐ, spoken of by Nöldeke (§ 328), it should be ܗܘܐ instead of the fem. ܗܘܬ. But I don't think it advisable to change the text, because to the Greek neuter correspond in Syriac both genders, masc. as well as fem.

Later on, p. 11, l. 22, we have again a fem. subject connected with a masc. verb ܟܪ̈ܬܐ [ܕܫܠܡܘܢ =] ܕܫܠܡܘ̱ܢ ܪ̈ܘܚܡܝܢ ܘܐܫܠܡܘܢ (Nöldeke, § 321 ; Duval, § 378 a).

On the stat. emph. p. 6, l. 21, ܬܗܘܐ ܛܒܐ ܘܫܦܝܪܐ = *καλὸς κἀγαθὸς γενόμενος*, comp. Nöldeke, 204 B, C.

p. 10, l. 3. ܡܢ ܣ̈ܢܝܬܐ. I have not changed the text, but it seems to stand for ܡܢ ܣܢܐܬܐ "from hatred."

As to the Lexicon, no wholly unknown word is contained in our text, except the proper names; but there are several, examples for which are highly welcome. For instance

ܒܣܒܣ = *σπαράττειν* [p. 5, l. 4]; Payne Smith 546; to the examples given there add Julian, ed. Hoffm. 57, 3[1].

ܒܨܪ [p. 11, l. 18] with the sense of *investigate*.

ܢܓܪܬܐ = *ζωγρεῖον* [p. 8, l. 19].

ܫܗܝܐ ܠܢܦܫܗܘ̱ܢ with the special sense *ναυτιάω* [p. 4, l. 1], for which compare Novaria 177 as quoted by Castle-Michaelis 895 = Lagarde Praetermissa 32, 31.

At the end I have put a list of some of the rarer words. Here I may yet mention ܡܢ ܟܐܕܢ [p. 12, l. 12] "as for

[1] I may be pardoned for seizing the opportunity of correcting an old mistake connected with this word. Beside ܒܣܒܣ and its infinitive-noun ܒܘܣܒܣܐ Bar Ali has (ed. Hoffmann 4647) ܟܘܣܟܣܐ ܕܓܪ̈ܡܐ (sic), Bar Bahlul (ed. Duval 3, 880) ܟܘܣܟܣܐ ܕܓܪ̈ܡܐ, the same Payne Smith 1786, Cardahi (al-Lobab 589). The two latter give as its meaning, on the authority of Karmsodinoyo, *cartilago*, it. *pars ossium medulosa quae mandi possit*; BA and BB acknowledge it as infinitive-noun with the meaning *abrodere ossa, exedere medullam*: it is clear that the whole paragraph is due to the misspelling ܟܘܣܟܣܐ instead of ܒܘܣܒܣܐ.

me" as a very good rendering of the Greek ᾤμην (347 B). Quite in the same way it stands Lag. An. 191, 21 for καὶ μὴν ἐδόκουν (περὶ ἀοργ. 872 F). This leads to the question as to the rendering of the Greek text.

Whether our tract has been rendered into Syriac by the same hand, to which we owe the Syriac version of περὶ ἀοργησίας (and περὶ ἀρετῆς) I dare not answer in a definite way; yet it seems to me very likely. The general treatment of the two texts is quite the same. Particulars, for instance, of Greek Mythology, unknown to the Syriac and Christian reader, are left out in both texts; so are uncommon proper names; instead of them we read "a king," "a wise man"; the vocabulary is very similar. It is a pity that in the beginning of περὶ ἀοργησίας the beautiful saying of Musonius is left untranslated: δεῖν ἀεὶ θεραπευομένους βιοῦν τοὺς σώζεσθαι μέλλοντας. For this latter expression occurs again in our tract in the saying of Antisthenes [p. 9, l. 11], ὅτι τοῖς μέλλουσι σώζεσθαι ἢ φίλων δεῖ γνησίων ἢ διαπύρων ἐχθρῶν, and our translator has given it here in a very singular way, quite destroying the almost Christian tinge which the word has in these and similar passages: he gives it ܪܐܘܡܝܐ ܐܠ ܪ‌ܐܡܘܝ ‌‌‌‌‌ܗܘܒܪ‌ܝܐ ‌‌‌ܪܠܝܬ *he who wishes to get famous by (in) his behaviour*[1].

But there is another passage, which is almost identical in both texts, the saying of Plato, that men must give a severe reckoning even of the lightest thing in the world, the uttered word. In περὶ ἀοργ. 456 D it runs thus: κουφοτάτου πράγματος, ὡς φησὶν ὁ Πλάτων, λόγου βαρυτάτην ζημίαν τίσουσιν ἐχθροὶ καὶ κακολόγοι καὶ κακοήθεις δοκοῦντες εἶναι. This is rendered in the Syriac (Lagarde, 189, 23):

ܘܙܝܐ ‌ܐܡܪ ܗܘܡ ܟܐ ‌ܘܠܦܐ ܕ‌ܠܬܐ ܡܚܬܪ‌ܝܐ

---

[1] On this use of σώζεσθαι the theological reader may compare Wyttenbach's Annotations to Plut., de discern. adul. ab amico, 74 C, p. 548.

ܕܐܝܬܝܗ ܨܒܘܬܐ ܩܠܝܠܬܐ ܡܣܬܒܪܢܝܬܐ ܕܢܬܒ ܡܫܬܠܡܝܢ ܒܒܥܠܕܒܒܐ ܡܢ ܐܠܗܐ ܘܡܢ ܒܢ̈ܝܢܫܐ ܡܛܠܬܗ i.e. and well has Platon said, that of the word, which is believed to be the lightest thing, *a heavy punishment shall receive the enemies from God and from men, because of it.*

In our tract (90 C) we have it in this form: λόγου δὲ, κουφοτάτου πράγματος, βαρυτάτη ζημία κατὰ τὸν θεῖον Πλάτωνα καὶ παρὰ θεῶν ἕπεται καὶ παρὰ ἀνθρώπων.

The corresponding Syriac is here: ܦܠܛܘܢ ܕܝܢ ܐܡܪ ܕܕܡܠܬܐ ܠܗ ܩܠܝܠܬܐ ܬܘܒܥܐ ܡܬܦܪܥܝܢ ܒܢ̈ܝ ܐܢܫܐ ܡܢ ܐܠܗܐ ܘܡܢ ܐܢܫܐ, "*But Plato said, that of the light(est) word men must pay loss by God and by man.*" That ζημία in this text is rendered by its second, or perhaps original, meaning *damnum, loss*, is remarkable; comp. for the Syriac ܬܘܒܥܐ beside the examples given by Castle-Michaelis, Julianus ed. Hoffm. 105, 8 ܬܘܒܥܐ ܘܚܘܣܪܢܐ; 186, 23; the verb 107, 25; 172, 25; ܦܘܪ̈ܥܢܐ ܘܬܘ̈ܒܥܐ Lag. Anal. 186, 2. Thus we might suppose two different translators; but on the other hand, the addition in the first text "*from God and man*," which has nothing there to correspond to it in the Greek, nor indeed in the passages of Plato referred to[1], seems best to be explained by the supposition that the translator of περὶ ἀοργησίας had the passage of our tract in mind; and this again would be most easily accounted for if it was one and the same person who translated both. In the Sinaitic MS. our tract stands first, then follows περὶ ἀσκήσεως, then "a discourse of Pythagoras" (probably the same as Lag. Anal. 195—201), then περὶ ἀοργησίας.

[1] Legg. 4, 717 C (601 D) διότι κούφων καὶ πτηνῶν λόγων βαρυτάτη ζημία· πᾶσι γὰρ ἐπίσκοπος τοῖς περὶ τὰ τοιαῦτα ἐτάχθη Δίκης Νέμεσις ἄγγελος, and 11, 935 A (684 B) ἐκ λόγων, κούφου πράγματος, ἔργῳ μίση τε καὶ ἔχθραι βαρύταται γίγνονται.

At what time and in what place these versions from the Greek philosopher were made, we are not informed; the other pieces contained in the Sinaitic MS. as well as in that of the British Museum 987 (Wright's Catalogue p. 1160) referred to by Harris (p. 5) should be compared with them. Edessa has always the first claims to be thought of.

As they are adaptations rather than literal translations their help for emendation of the present Greek text is not very great. Immediately at the beginning of our tract there is a crux interpretum : it has: Ὁρῶ μὲν, ὅτι τὸν πραότατον, ὦ Κορνήλιε Πούλχερ, ἄτερ πολιτείας ᾔρησαι τρόπον. Instead of ἄτερ, one MS. has ὅπερ, others proposed ἄτε δή. The Syriac has merely: "Because I see thee, Cornelius, that it is chosen by thee, to lead the meekest life." He leaves the doubtful word out and read perhaps ὁρῶν μὲν, to which participle in the Greek δοκεῖ μοι in l. 10 with an anacoluthon or ἀπέσταλκά σοι would form the sequel.

But there is at least one passage where the current Greek text receives an undoubted emendation from the Syriac.

On p. 88 C (339) we have the following connexion :

Εἰ θέλεις ἀνιᾶν τὸν μισοῦντα, μὴ λοιδόρει κίναιδον... ἀλλ᾽ αὐτὸς ἀνὴρ ἴσθι καὶ σωφρόνει...ἂν δὲ λοιδορῆσαι προαχθῇς, ἄπαγε πορρωτάτω σεαυτὸν ὧν λοιδορεῖς ἐκεῖνον... μή τις καὶ σοί ποθεν ὑποφθέγγηται κακία τὸ τοῦ τραγῳδοῦ·

ἄλλων ἰατρὸς αὐτὸς ἕλκεσι βρύων·

ἂν ἀπαίδευτον εἴπῃ σε, ἐπίτεινε τὸ φιλομαθὲς ἐν σεαυτῷ καὶ φιλόπονον· ἂν δειλὸν, ἔγειρε μᾶλλον τὸ θαρσαλέον καὶ ἀνδρῶδες...οὐδὲν γὰρ αἴσχιόν ἐστι βλασφημίας παλινδρομούσης καὶ λυπηρότερον.

Every careful reader will perceive from the connexion, that the sense must be: *if thou callest him a fool*, not *if he calls thee so*: *si eum illiteratum dicis*, not *si te dicit*; that

we, therefore, with the slightest change must read: ἂν
ἀπαίδευτον εἴπῃς, ἐπίτεινε.   It is strange that Wyttenbach
(or Xylander before him? see the preface of Wyttenbach,
p. 142) gives the right sense in the translation, but did not
receive it into the text nor mention it in the annotations.
Whether it was done in later editions, I have not the means
of ascertaining here.   Again on p. 91 F (353) where in the
received text is mentioned a πολιτικὸς ἀνὴρ 'Ονομάδημος ἐν
Χίῳ, our version calls him Δῆμος, read therefore ὄνομα
Δῆμος (or τοὔνομα) with the authorities alleged by Wyttenbach in the annotations p. 635.

While, as a rule, the Greek text is abbreviated by the
Syriac author, there is one passage, where the latter has a
little amplification.   Omitting the sentence (91 F) that it
is useful to the man τῶν παθῶν ποιούμενος ἀποκαθάρσεις
εἰς τοὺς ἐχθροὺς καὶ ἀποστρέφων ὥσπερ ὀχετούς, he says
instead of this not very friendly comparison, that we must
have frequent resort to the house of the wise men, as to
those of the physicians.   Did he not like the comparison or
not understand it?   But the relation of the Greek Original
to the Syriac will be best seen by the annexed version.   I
have purposely made it as literal to the Syriac as possible,
and have nothing to add but my best thanks to Prof.
J. Rendel Harris, who to his kindness of handing over
to me his Syriac copy has joined that of revising my
English and of providing that the whole could be printed.

E. NESTLE.

ULM, *August*, 1893.

A TRACT OF PLUTARCH ON THE ADVAN-
TAGE TO BE DERIVED BY A MAN FROM
HIS ENEMY.

BECAUSE I see, Cornelius, that thou hast chosen for
thyself to walk in meekness, so that, whilst thou art
helping the common affairs, thou in thy own person
shewest hardness to no man; and again because, as the
writers say, there is not to be found in the land of Crete
any wild beast, but no community of men is to be found,
even in modern times, free from envy and jealousy and
strife, which are the springs of enmity : yet how often
friendship is wont to produce on the other side enmity,
as also Chilon the wise pointed out! For when he was
told that a certain man had no enemy, he answered and
said 'and therefore no friend.' For he was persuaded
that it was right for a man to know how the affairs of
enemies stand; and it was not in vain that Xenophon
said that 'it is the mark of a wise man that he knows
how to profit by his enemies.'

For lo! to them of old time it was enough if only
they were not hurt by wild beasts, and this single con-
sideration was the end in view in their fight against them :
but those who came after and learned their use, took
advantage of their bodies for food, and of their hair for
clothing; and for healing, too, they took matter from
them; they armed themselves with their claws, and covered
themselves with their hides; so that in consequence of this

it is to be feared that when the beasts have disappeared from our life, our own life may become as that of the beasts, in which resources will not be found, though wildness may be.

Now since for most men it suffices that their enemies do them no damage, but Xenophon, on the other hand, said that they are very profitable to the wise man (and on this point one must not doubt); we will examine how this advantage is to be found. For the examination of it is needful for us, who cannot live without enemies. For the gardener cannot change every tree for the better, nor again is it easy for the hunter to tame all beasts; yet they understand how by certain means to derive profit from wild things: and we may see the planter deriving advantage from fruitless trees, and the hunter from wild beasts. The waters of the sea are salt and very bitter, but they grow fish at all parts of their depths and conduct merchants on their waves. Fire, again, burns him who comes near to it, but it shews light and diffuses warmth, and is the means for all handicrafts that know how to use it. See if the enemy be not like to these in that while in one direction a man approaches him warily, in others he fulfils our need and is profitable. And we may see many things which, while they are antagonistic to us and hurt us, are in other respects useful to us. How many have fallen into bodily sickness, and their sickness has humbled them and restrained them from evil! How many have fallen on toil, and the toil has given strength and hardness to their members; others have been deprived of their country and their fortunes, and they have made use of both losses as food for the journey, and they became 'to them the means of rest and of useful occupation, as in the case of Diogenes and Crates. Zeno, when he heard that the ship, which had been sent by him to sea, had been wrecked, answered and said : 'It is well for me, so that I may turn to philosophy.' For as those animals whose stomachs are sound, if they eat snails or scorpions, digest them ; and as others feed on pebbles and clay, and through the warmth of their stomachs, digest them ; but those, whose stomach is weak, become ill even if they get sustenance of bread and wine ; in the same way the fools are wont even by friendship to get damage, while the wise profit by enmity, making good use of it.

For lo! that which is considered the most difficult, is for the discriminating the most profitable; it is this ; he (the enemy) searches out thy ways of living and does not sleep from examining thy steps and trying to find a cause against thee, while he turns hither and thither; therefore watchfulness does not hurt thee, but recalls thee to useful behaviour. For the enemy does not make his inquisition carelessly ; for his gaze enters, as it were, through the walls of thy house, and his spy pierces the stones of thy dwelling, yea! he plunders the very mind of thy friends, and through thy neighbours he spies out thy works and gets thy secrets from the midst of thy beloved by gifts which he offers them. For people are very often, through carelessness, in the habit of not noticing even the death of their friends : but enemies enquire even about the things that they see in their dreams. And if illness come upon a man, or if he takes a loan or has a quarrel with his wife, his enemies perceive it before his friends. But especially their glance keeps to the failings of their foes, and from all quarters they search them out. And as the vultures by scent are gathered on carcases, while they do not at all perceive sound bodies ; so also enemies come down and gather on evil ways and dead deeds, and draw near to them and tear them. And this is profitable ; yea! beloved, it is great profit, that we become watchful over our ways and examine

our persons and do nothing carelessly and say nothing
thoughtlessly, but that we be blameless in all our steps, for
herein the danger lies. By chastising our passions and
warning our thoughts he increases in us the study to live
soberly and without reproof. For as towns against which
war is raised by their neighbours and against which armies
advance, are constantly weaned from their evil customs and
are governed according to law instead of being in revolution, thus also many are reproved by reason of enmity:
they become awake and watchful and are not ready to
do anything lightly, and by and by they learn not to fail
again and they adorn themselves with virtue and are
alarmed even at blame. For every thing, in which the
enemies rejoice, if it comes to their heart, holds them back
from them and their deeds[1]. We see also those who play
on the lyre, that when one of them plays by himself in
the theatre, he often employs his art carelessly: but when
he goes down to the contest against the other players, his
fellows, then he not only recalls his mind from wandering,
but he awakens and strengthens also the strings of his lyre
and puts them in good order for the contest. Thus also
must he who is conscious that he is going down into the
battle with his enemies in order to conquer them by his
prowess or that they may conquer him, watch especially
over himself and like that player on the lyre see to himself
and his deeds.

For this also is a mark of evil that a man is more
ashamed when he sins before his enemies than before his
friends: as also a wise man signifies; for when it was
said to him that the affairs of the Romans must be in
safety, since they had subdued and conquered their enemies,
he answered and said: Now there is great danger since

---

[1] The Syriac is not clear.

there is not left them any before whom they might be
ashamed. But understand, dear friend, the word which
Diogenes said, which is very wise and helpful. For when
he was asked by someone how to avenge himself on his
enemies, he answered and said to him: Thus canst thou
avenge thyself, by becoming good and honest. For if they
feel grieved when they see the horses of those against whom
they have hatred to be praised, or his dogs or his garden,
what will they do when the man himself is praised and
when everybody declares his righteousness and sobriety
and wisdom and the care over his ways, in that he gathers
fruit from the deep furrows of his mind whence spring
all the thoughts that are full of righteousness? And
another wise man has said that the enemies are brought
to silence, not merely as such, nor all of them, but according as they see that their enemies are sober and good and
merciful towards them. For these virtues are a bridle to
their tongues, and shut their mouths and direct them to
quietness. And thou, therefore, if thou wishest to do harm
to thy enemy, do not call him voluptuous or a liar or an
impertinent fellow, but shew thyself in thy own person
the contrary of it, and be cautious and true and merciful
and righteous towards every man. But if thou art also
provoked to blame him, be thyself far from the blame
which thou layest upon him: enter into thy mind, and
examine thy deeds[1], lest thou hear from these that thou art
a physician whilst thou art full of sores. If also thou callest
him a fool, do thou thyself add and win wisdom; if a coward,
multiply thou courage; and if thou callest him voluptuous,
buffet thou the lusts that are in thy own mind. For there
is nothing which is more hateful and distressing, than a
reproach which falls back on him that sent it; and as

---

[1] Did he read περισκόπει τὰ σὰ ἔργα instead of τὰ σαθρά?

weak eyes are hurt by light, that falls on a place and is reflected upon them, so also a blame, when it reflects from without a truth on him that has uttered it, he who sent it forth is vexed thereby. And Plato, when he saw men that were vile, was wont to say as he turned away from them: 'Lest I myself were to become so.' He, therefore, who reproaches his neighbour, when he turns to him and sees himself, as in an example, is himself also helped by the reproach which he cast, though it is [otherwise] very damaging. But most men laugh when they see a man who, while he is bald or hump-backed, reproaches others with those faults. But many fools reproach others with what turns back on themselves. Leo, however, when he was called blind by one who had a hump, answered and said to him: Thou reproachest me with a bodily defect, but thou bearest thy defects upon thy shoulders. Therefore do not call thy neighbour an adulterer, while thou thyself art sensual; nor licentious, while thou art impertinent. Domitius wished to reproach Crassus, who, when an animal died that he had kept in a cage, had wept about it; but Crassus said to him: 'That I might not be like thyself; thou hast buried three wives that thou hast had, and hast not wept for one of them.' But this is not required, that a man be ready for slandering and daring and raising his voice, but that, while he reproaches, he does not give opportunity that the reproach be sent back to himself. For this also God demands from any who wishes to reproach his neighbour, that he first examine himself, lest while he says what pleases him, he should hear what does not rejoice him, and lest his ears should unwillingly perceive what his mouth has sent forth willingly.

This, therefore, is the advantage of the man that reproaches his enemies: but there is also another advantage to be found, in that a man be reproached by his enemies. Therefore rightly Antisthenes said : He whose object is that he be famous in his conduct, has need either of true friends or of mighty enemies, inasmuch as they, by chastising him when he has sinned and by reproaching him, turn him away from that which is foul. But because the voice of love is feeble[1] and cannot reprehend with a full mouth, but is ready for sweet words : it is necessary therefore that we should hear the truth from our enemies. For like as Telephus, who had no physician, brought the sore of his complaint under the lance of his enemy, so must he who has no friend to reprehend him, tolerate the reprehension of his enemies, when they reprehend and unveil his vices, looking on the healing that he gets, and not on the mind that is working him ill. For like the man whom from hatred some one wished to kill, and struck him with the sword on a tumour, and thus, through this stroke, as through an incision, the tumour was opened and he saved from death ; so often from anger or from enmity a reproach is uttered, and a pain, that is hidden or covered in the soul, is made whole. But most people, when they are reproached, do not look whether the reproach be true or not, but they look for some other word by which he who reproaches them may be reproached : after the fashion of athletes, who go down to fight, who do not at all wipe away what is thrown upon them, but turn and throw again ; thus also do these defile each other with reproaches in their fight with one another. But we ought, when we are reproached by our enemies, if it is a true word, to keep our soul from it and not leave the sore that was shewn to us : but, if it be not true, we must seek the cause from which this reproach was taken : but we must

---

[1] *Lit.* extinguished.

fear and be cautious, in case we have transgressed or done something like or similar to what was said: a thing which happened also to that king of Argos; for the hair of the locks of his head, and a lazy manner of walking, brought upon him a foul suspicion. Again there came upon Pompeius from a certain cause a similar reproach, though he was far from lasciviousness. Moreover Crassus was reproached on account of a virgin. For, because he wished to buy from her a parcel of ground, he was obliged to write to her and to honour her. And for Postumia inordinate laughter and freedom of speech gained the reproach of licentiousness, so that she was accused of adultery: but she was found innocent. The judge, however, warned her and told her not to use words at all that are foreign to modesty. Themistocles, too, though he was pure, and no traitor of the town, fell into a suspicion of treachery because he constantly received letters from his friend Pausanias. When therefore a word is spoken that is not true, we must not, because it is a false rumour, despise and contemn it, but we must search and see, whether in our speech or in our deeds, or in those who are attached to us, there be found anything that is like the rumour. We must avoid and flee from it.

For if to most people the losses that befell them increased their knowledge, as also Merope said: 'misfortunes have taken from me my friends and have taught me caution': what hinders us from setting up for ourselves constantly a teacher, free of charge, and learning from him what is hidden in our own mind? For the enemy perceives many things, of which the friend is not conscious. For, as Plato said, he who loves is blind as regards seeing the faults of his friends. But hatred, while his glance is keen, has also his mouth open. Hieron when he quarrelled with his enemy was reproached by him for the foulness of the smell of his mouth. Then, when he came to his house, he answered and said to his wife: neither hast thou told me the defect that is upon me.' But she, because she had not had intercourse with another man, and was innocent, answered and said to him: 'as for me, I believed that such was the smell of the mouth of all men.' Thus it is easy to learn known faults and secret faults first from enemies, before we learn them from friends and lovers.

And without this it is not possible for us to restrain our tongue and gain, without much exercise, that great part of the righteousness which a man must have in order to subdue his passions which love noise and talkativeness which are the cause of quarrelsomeness and enmity. For if it happens that our tongue trespasses with a word: it flies like a bird from our nests; and from the mouth of a man who is not practised in subduing his anger there often fly words[1], and from his weakness and carelessness and impertinence he stumbles. But Plato said that of the lightest word people must pay damages both to God and man. But silence not only, as the physicians say, keeps from thirst, but also from reprehensions and rebukes. There is nothing more honourable than that a man when he is reproached by his enemy should keep silence. For if thou art silent towards him, it is much more easy for thee to endure thy wife, if she speaks ill of thee: and the brother, too, and the friend, thou canst tolerate when they reproach thee. And, further, thou dost endure without anger thy father and thy mother, even when they beat thee. For Isocrates (sic!) took a hard and passionate wife in order that it might be easy for him to bear with strangers, having been exercised by her in patience. It is, however, much

---

[1] Remark the idiomatic expression تخلم تخلم.

better that a man should be exercised by his enemies, and
practised by their reproaches and their railing, and that
he restrain his anger and do not suffer it to arise when
reviling provokes it.

Meekness, therefore, and patience, we must thus shew
towards enemies, but [also we must shew] simplicity
and sweetness and goodness, even more than towards
friends. For it is not so much a great thing, if we do
good to our friend, as it is a shameful thing, if we
do it not. But as regards one's enemy, if a man forbears
vengeance, when it was easy for him to avenge, this is a
mark of goodness: but if he weeps over his fall and
stretches out his hand towards his need and shews kindly
care with goodwill towards his children or towards his
relatives, when he sees them in need: who would not
love such an one and praise his peacefulness and his goodness, whose heart he sees to be made as of iron and
diamond! When Caesar ordered to re-erect the statues
of Pompeius his enemy, that had been thrown down, a
wise man answered and said: Those statues thou hast
re-erected, but thine own thou hast fastened. Therefore
we must neither spare praise nor honour, if it is due to
any one who is our enemy. For he is more praised who
praises his enemy, and through this there is room that
his reproof be believed, when he reproves, as of one who
does not hate the man, but repudiates his deeds. And
what is the best of all, is that it is observed concerning
him that he is very far from envying the valor of his
friends, because he often praised his enemies. For through
this he shews, that still less is he becoming envious, because
his friends succeed. And lo! what study can be better
than this, that a man should gain the mind that eradicates
envy and jealousy from his soul? For like as those who
are accustomed to war are possessed by the passion of

anger, and it is, therefore, not easy for them to repress it
during peace, though it is damaging, because it is rooted
in them with other passions, that are fit for war, but not
useful in peace, so is it with enmity, which brings in with
the hatred envy and jealousy and causes a man to rejoice
in evil and to keep wrath, while he is cunning and full of
tricks and ready to do hurt. For all this, when it is used
against enemies, does not appear very hard: but it is
treasured in the soul and from custom a man is led to
use it also against his friends, and he does wrong to his
beloved, if he is not careful towards his enemies. Therefore one of the philosophers, that he might accustom
himself to be friendly towards men, shewed mercifulness
towards animals.

For it is very honourable, if we have enmity against a
man, that we also in the time of our anger walk righteously
toward him and do not deceive our enemy, and be not
cunning in evil, so that it may be possible for us to be
free from falsity in our love to our friends. Scaurus was
an enemy of Domitius. There came a slave of Domitius
privately to open the secrets of his master to his enemy
Scaurus. But Scaurus did not allow him to open his
mouth, but took him and sent him to his master. Now
this not only brings praise, but is also very advantageous.
For if we accustom ourselves to be righteous towards our
enemies, we shall be in no wise wicked towards our friends.
Now because there comes on us envy and strife, it is
proper that when we suffer from them, we should go to the
doors of the wise, as to the doors of the physicians, and
through useful words extinguish the flame. But when a
man has to bear great evils from his enemies, the word
will come to his heart, which the wise Demos has spoken.
For this man was very fond of his friends, and he was
noble in his words: when now a revolution took place

in his town, and his party was victorious, he began to
counsel and to say: And, my comrades, we will not destroy
all our enemies, but leave a residue of them, lest if these
disappeared from us, we should begin to do harm to ourselves. So ought we to do : if there are in us evil passions,
we will exhaust them in endurance against our enemies,
that we may not in the least do harm to our friends. For
it must not be, that things should be, as Hesiod speaks of;
for he says the potter envies the potter, and the neighbour
the neighbour, and again the sons of brothers envy each
other. But if it is not easy for a man to be free from envy,
I counsel that he subdue it[1] towards his enemies, and not[2]
envy them[3] when they succeed, that he may be able to be
without envy towards his friends. For like as the rose-
gardeners believe, that the rose or the lily become more
beautiful, when they plant beside them onions and garlic ;
for they suck up all foulness and sharpness ; so also the
enemy sucks up all our bitterness and makes us to be
pleasant to our friends. Therefore we must become like
them in their ability and emulate them in their virtue,
and not grudge them their successes, and understand from
what causes they excel, and be zealous to surpass them
through carefulness, keeping an eye on our own selves
and walking cautiously: as also Themistocles said : that
the victory which Miltiades gained does not allow him to
sleep. For he who envies the successes of his enemies and

[1] So the MS.

[2] So again MS.

[3] It is strange that, as stated by Wyttenbach : "Stephanus dedit
δάκνεσθαι μὴ τῶν ἐχθρῶν : perperam μὴ arripiens ex Pol. et Jannot.
Abest recte ab Ald. Bas. Xyl. A. B. E. Mosc. 1. 2." Did the Syriac
author also find a negation in his MS.? The Greek text of Wyttenbach is ἀλλ' εἰ μηδεὶς τρόπος ἐστὶν [sic] ἄλλος ἀπαλλαγῆς ἐρίδων καὶ
φθόνων καὶ φιλονεικῶν, ἔθιζε σαυτὸν δάκνεσθαι τῶν ἐχθρῶν εὐημερούντων,
καὶ παρόξυνε καὶ χάραττε τὸ φιλόνεικον ἐν ἐκείνοις θηγόμενον.

at once plunges himself in grief uses his envy as an idle thing. But he whose eyes are not blind, profits by him whom he envies, by seeing that most of his results are gained by zeal and carefulness, so that in lifting his glance upon them, he is benefited by imitating them, and he casts from him his sleep and his idleness. But if he sees in them disquiet and subtilty, or that they judge without righteousness, or gain fortune by shameful means, he is not at all angry at this; but perhaps his mind rejoices, that through comparison with them his candour will be recognised. As Plato said: All the gold that is found on the earth and in the midst of the earth, does not weigh against the gloriousness of conduct, according to what Solon said: We in no wise exchange virtuous behaviour for riches, nor for the praises of drunken spectators, nor to obtain honour with eunuchs and concubines and satraps of kings. For there is nothing that is enviable and virtuous that sprang from a shameful cause. But because the faults[1] of our friends are not seen by us, but the vices of our enemies we quickly perceive, we must not rejoice, even if we are inclined to, when they fall, nor be distressed when they succeed, nor stay unprofitably in either the one or the other: but from their vices we must guard ourselves, and their virtues we must imitate, so that by watchfulness against the evil we may surpass and conquer our enemies, and in the imitation of their virtues we may not fail nor fall behind.

Endeth the tract of Plutarch on the advantage to be derived by a man from his enemy.

---

[1] According to the Greek τυφλοῦται τὸ φιλοῦν περὶ τὸ φιλούμενον we expect instead of ܪܚܡܘܬܐ something like ܪܚܡܝܢ.

INDEX OF SOME SYRIAC WORDS WITH THEIR GREEK EQUIVALENTS.

ܙܗܪ, ܡܙܗܪ p. 5, l. 11; videtur esse part. Pael (invito puncto, non Afel) ut ܡܩܦܣܝܢ l. 10; contra ܡܦܩܠܟܐ l. 11 Afel

ܙܘܕܐ ἐφόδιον p. 3, l. 14

ܙܢܘܢ Ζήνων p. 3, l. 16

ܙܠܠ, ܙܠܠܘܬܐ p. 7, ll. 10, 20, κίναιδος or μαλακός; p. 11, l. 5, θηλύτης καὶ ἀκολασία.

ܚܒ̈ܘܪܬܐ ἕλκη p. 7, l. 17

ܚܣܢ (Pael) ῥώννυμι p. 3, l. 11; ἀκριβέστερον ἁρμόζειν p. 6, l. 4

ܚܛܘܛܐ αὖλαξ p. 7, l. 1

ܚܠܢ διερευνᾶν p. 4, l. 13

ܚܨ̈ܦܐ ὄστρακα p. 3, l. 21

ܚܪܡܐ ἀνελεύθερος p. 8, l. 18

ܚܫܝܠ κεχάλκευται p. 14, l. 4

ܛܘܠܝܡ εὐφυής p. 8, l. 23

ܛܠܠܦܘܣ Τήλεφος p. 9, l. 18

ܟܘܕܪ̈ܐ γύπες p. 4, l. 23

ܟܘܣ φείδω p. 14, l. 8

ܟܘܣܬܢܐ κύρτος p. 8, l. 14

ܟܝܠܘܢ Χίλων p. 1, l. 13

ܟܘܫܪܐ ܕܒܢܝ ܐܢܫܐ πολιτεία p. 1, l. 8

ܟܣܢܘܦܘܢ Ξενοφῶν p. 1, l. 17; p. 2, l. 11

ܠܐܘܢ Λέων p. 8, l. 13

ܠܘܣ ἅπτεσθαι p. 3, l. 1

ܡܘܡܐ [ἴδιον] p. 6, l. 10

ܡܘܪܦܐ Μερόπη p. 11, l. 22

ܡܠܛܝܕܣ Μιλτιάδης p. 17, l. 15

ܡܠܝܢ (ἄποτος) p. 2, l. 22

ܕܘܟܪܢܝܬ ܟܐ ܕܘܟܘܣܝ p. 5, l. 15 εὐνομία καὶ πολιτεία ὑγιαίνουσα

ܟܘܝܢ ἀκόλαστος, ἄσωτος p. 7, l. 11; p. 8, l. 17

ܡܫܟܐ δέρμα p. 2, l. 5

ܟܕܝܢ ζωγρεῖον p. 8, l. 19

ܟܣܝܛܦܐ σατράπαι p. 18, l. 11

ܣܠܐ Σόλων p. 18, l. 8

ܣܩܪܘܣ Σκαῦρος p. 15, ll. 18, 20, 21

ܐܣܬܬܬ fundari p. 15, l. 1

ܡܕܝܢܝ πολιτικός p. 6, l. 18

ܡܕܢܐ (ἡ τῶν ὀμμάτων ἀσθένεια) p. 8, l. 13

ܒܕ ܝܚ ܟ ἄκων, opp. ܒܕ ܨܒ ܟ = ἑκών p. 9, l. 5

ܨܘܪ ܟܡܣ κόμης διάθεσις p. 11, l. 1

ܩܠܕ, ܩܠܕܟ [ἄγχειν, ἐγκράτεια] p. 7, l. 7; p. 12, l. 16

ܩܒܪ περιοδεύειν p. 4, l. 8

ܩܒܠ aberratio p. 6, l. 3

ܦܠܘܛܪܣ, ܦܠܘܛܪܣ Πλούταρχος: init. et fin.

ܦܫܝܩܘܬ loquacitas p. 12, l. 19

ܟܬܕܦܠܠ συμπάσσουσιν ἀλλήλους p. 10, l. 16

ܦܠܛܐ Πλάτων p. 8, l. 3; p. 12, ll. 4, 24; p. 18,
l. 6

ܦܡܦܝܐ, ܦܡܦܝܐ Πομπήιος p. 11, l. 3; p. 14, l. 6

ܦܣܢܝܐ Παυσανίας p. 11, l. 14

ܦܘܣܬܘܡܝܐ Ποστουμία (notice ܬ, not ܛ) p. 11, l. 7

ܡܢ ܟܐܪܝ ᾠόμην p. 12, l. 12

ܨܢܝܥܘ (ἀπάτη, ἐπιβουλή), cunning p. 15, l. 5

ܨܒܝ παιδομανής p. 8, l. 17

ܩܒܠܐ, ܩܒܠ ἐγκαλεῖν p. 14, l. 12

ܩܘܪܢܠܝܘ Κορνήλιος p. 1, l. 3

ܩܬܕܡܠ, ܟܠܐ [ἀνιᾶσθαι, ἐπιστένειν] p. 6, l. 23

ܩܣܪ   Καῖσαρ   p. 14, l. 5

ܩܪܛܝܣ   Κράτης   p. 3, l. 15

ܩܪܣܘܣ   Κράσσος   p. 8, ll. 18, 20; p. 11, l. 5

ܫܢܝ ܕܡܫܬܒܩ   ναυτιάω   p. 4, l. 1

ܫܘܡܬܐ   sore (κηλίς): p. 10, l. 19; cf. Jos. Styl. 21, 17,
ed. Wr.; Julian, ed. Hoffm. 57, 21

ܫܝܫ   continere, lenire   p. 3, l. 10

ܫܝܫܐ   ἴα   p. 17, l. 5

ܫܘܢܝܐ   φῦμα   p. 10, l. 5

ܫܝܠ   (Ethp.) προάγεσθαι   p. 7, l. 13

ܫܝܠ   ὀλισθάνειν   p. 12, l. 23

ܫܝܪܬܐ   ἁμαρτίαι   p. 4, l. 22

ܬܒܪܐ   πράγματα ἀβούλητα   p. 11, l. 20

ܬܘܡܐ   κρόμμυα   p. 17, l. 6

ܬܟܠܬܐ   ἐν ἀσφαλεῖ   p. 6, l. 13

Fol. 112 r, col. b

 || ‌.
_____

[1] Cod. ‌

.[1] ||

 ||

---

[1] Sic Cod., an ?   [2] Cod.

[3] Cod.

: Fol. 111 v, col. a
---

[1] Cod.

 || 15
---

[1] Cod. ; si ad femin. , non ad masc.
 verbum referendum esset, esset *estat-*
tetat.

     Fol. 110 v, col. b

     Fol. 111 r, col. a

---

¹ Cod.

 || :
Fol. 110 r, col. b

10

15

Fol. 110 v, col. a
 || .

20

---

[1] Cod.

 ||
 Fol. 109 v, col. b
15 ||
 Fol. 110 r, col. a

 || Fol. 109r, col. a
 || Fol. 109r, col. b
---

[1] Cod.

[Syriac text, Fol. 108 v, col. a and col. b]

1 Cod. ܪܠܐ ܕܚܢܝܟܐ   2 Cod. ܩܠܝܬܐ

3 Cod. ܠܬܟܠܐ

 Fol. 108 r, col. b
---

[1] Cod.

 ||

 || :

---

[1] Cod.

 ‹Fol. 107 r, col. b›
20 : ‹Fol. 107 v, col. a›

 ||
 ||

10 || ⟨Fol. 106ᵛ, col. a⟩
---

¹ Cod.

Fol. 106 r, col. a

Fol. 106 r, col. b

―――――――――

1 Cod.

 . ||
---

[1] Cod.   [2] Cod.   [3] Cod.

 ٥ا

www.ingramcontent.com/pod-product-compliance
Ingram Content Group UK Ltd.
Pitfield, Milton Keynes, MK11 3LW, UK
UKHW012021280225
455719UK00011B/420